Air Brakes
Prep Exam
Booklet

About Mile One Press

Helping students and commercial drivers study to pass CDL exams and receive CDL permits and endorsements.

Our Mission

To provide above industry-standard resources to help aspiring and professional commercial drivers take their first or next step in advancing their commercial driving careers.

Everything starts with you

We are obsessed with helping our customers improve their CDL pass rates. We know how a CDL certification or endorsement can transform your future. It did ours. So, we never stop working to improve our resources to ensure you can make your mark in this lucrative, in-demand career path.

CDL study resources designed for you

CDL prep starts here. Serving teachers, trainers, and students, we design study materials and resources to power improved CDL passes. While we can't guarantee a pass, we know our resources significantly boost your chances when used the right way.

Found out more at www.mileonepress.com

Advancing Commercial Driving Careers

The commercial driver industry is fast-growing yet continuously faced with a shortage of certified CDL drivers. Certification starts with passing the CDL written exam and that's where many fall short. We aim to change that trend. We also aim to enhance the learning experience of new commercial drivers and improve their driving capabilities.

The beginning of a new career path in the transportation industry starts with the CDL test. We're here to help you or your students over that speed bump and onto the next mile.

Our Philosophy

Education	**Integrity**	**Drive**	**Innovation**
Providing resources and teaching students to improve outcomes	Operating at the highest standards and adhering to our principles	Helping others to successfully move in the direction of their dreams	Continuous improvement for the best online CDL study platform

Table of Contents

Air Brakes Answers & Explained

Air Brakes Practice Exam 1 (25 Points)

1. **Oil and water usually collect in compressed air tanks. If you do not have an automatic tank drain, when should you drain the air tanks?**

   A. After every four hours of service.

   B. After every working day.

   C. Once a week.

2. **What is the S-cam used for?**

   A. To release the brakes.

   B. To test the slack adjusters.

   C. To apply the brakes.

3. **Which of the following makes the total stopping distance for air brakes longer than for hydraulic brakes?**

   A. Perception distance.

   B. Reaction distance.

   C. Brake lag distance.

4. **The brake system that applies and releases the brakes when the driver uses the brake pedal is the:**

   A. Emergency brake system.

   B. Service brake system.

   C. Parking brake system.

5. **To make an emergency stop with air brakes, using the stab braking method, you should:**

   A. Pump the brake pedal rapidly and lightly.

   B. Brake as hard as you can, get off the brakes when the wheels lock, get back on the brakes when the wheels start rolling again.

   C. Brake hard until the wheels lock, and then get off the brakes for as much time as the wheels were locked.

6. **Brake lag distance at 55 mph is _____ feet?**

   A. 50

   B. 23

   C. 32

7. **If your vehicle has an alcohol evaporator, it is there to:**

   A. Rid the wet tank of alcohol that condenses and sits at the bottom.

   B. Eliminate the need for daily tank draining.

   C. Reduce the risk of ice in air brake valves in cold weather.

8. **What can legally hold parking or emergency brake in position for a truck, truck tractor, or bus?**

   A. Fluid pressure

   B. Spring pressure

   C. Air pressure

9. **The braking power of the spring brakes:**

   A. Increases when the service brakes are hot.

   B. Depends on the adjustment of the service brakes.

   C. Is not affected by the condition of the service brakes.

10. **Which of the following should you do before leaving your vehicle unattended?**

    A. Set the parking brakes.

    B. Remove the keys.

    C. Chock the wheels.

    D. Do all of the above.

11. **Under which conditions are front-wheel brakes good?**

    A. None

    B. All weather conditions

    C. Wet or icy conditions only

    D. Good weather only

12. **If the air tanks are not drained,**

    A. your transmission fluid may drain out.

    B. Your brakes may fail because of the water freezing.

    C. You will drive too quickly.

    D. Your left side brake will cease to operate.

13. **An antilock braking system (ABS)**

    A. Increases your normal braking capability.

    B. Activates when your wheels are about to lock up.

    C. Decreases your normal braking capability.

    D. Shortens your stopping distance.

14. **Which of the following can cause brakes to fade or fail?**

    A. Excessive use of the service brakes

    B. Not relying enough on the engine braking

    C. Brakes being out of adjustment

    D. All of the above

15. **What is the best way to test if your vehicle's spring brakes come on automatically?**

    A. Continue to step on and off the brake pedal until the manufacturer's low psi specification is met for spring brakes to deploy.

    B. On single vehicles, continue to step on and off the brake pedal until the parking brake valve pops out.

    C. On tractor-trailer vehicles, continue to step on and off the brake pedal until the parking brake valve pops out.

    D. All of the above are correct.

16. **If your vehicle has a properly functioning dual air brake system and minimum-sized air tanks, the air pressure should build from 85 to 100 psi within _____ seconds.**

    A. 60

    B. 20

    C. 45

17. **The air compressor will stop pumping air into the air tanks at _____ psi.**

    A. 125

    B. B.150

    C. 100

18. **Excessive heat caused by overuse of the service brakes can cause**

    A. the modulating control valve to wear out.

    B. The brakes fade.

    C. The brake linings split.

19. **Excessive use of the service brakes may result in overheating, leading to**

    A. expansion of the brake drums.

    B. Improper adjustment of the S-cams.

    C. Increased contact between the brake drums and the brake linings.

20. **A typical air brake system is fully charged at**

    A. 150 psi.

    B. 75 psi.

    C. 125 psi.

21. **During normal driving, spring brakes are usually held back by**

    A. bolts and braces.

    B. Springs.

    C. Air pressure.

22. **During your final air brake check, if the air pressure does not build up fast enough,**

    A. the air pressure may drop too low during driving.

    B. Have the problem fixed after your trip is over.

    C. The alcohol evaporator may be low.

23. **To test the static air leakage rate, you should**

    A. turn off the engine, release the parking brake, and let the system settle.

    B. Charge the air system and leave the engine running.

    C. Leave the engine running and release the parking brake.

24. **Air brakes use _____ to make the brakes work.**

    A. hydraulic fluid

    B. compressed air

    C. natural gas

25. **When you press the brake pedal,**

    A. compressed air enters the brake chambers.

    B. Compressed air is released from the air tanks.

    C. Compressed air is released from the brake chambers.

Air Brakes Practice Exam 2

1. **The air compressor governor controls:**

   A. The speed of the air compressor.

   B. Air pressure was applied to the brakes.

   C. When air is pumped into the air tanks.

2. **Of the choices below, the first thing to do when a low air pressure warning comes on is:**

   A. Stop and safely park as soon as possible.

   B. Upshift.

   C. Adjust the brake pedal for more travel.

3. **Air brake equipped vehicles must have:**

   A. An air use gauge.

   B. A supply pressure gauge.

   C. At least two brake heaters.

4. **Modern air brake systems combine three different systems. They are the service brakes, the parking brakes, and the:**

   A. Emergency brakes.

   B. Foot brakes.

   C. S-cam brakes.

5. **If you must make an emergency stop, you should brake so that you:**

   A. Can steer hard while braking hard.

   B. Use the full power of the brakes and lock them.

   C. Stay in a straight line and can steer.

6. **The driver must be able to see a warning that is given before air pressure in the service air tanks falls below:**

   A. 20 psi

   B. 40 psi

   C. 60 psi

7. **The most common type of foundation brakes found on heavy vehicles is the:**

   A. Disc brakes

   B. Wedge drum

   C. S-cam brake

8. **When driving down a long steep hill, you should:**

   A. Release the brake when you are 5 mph below your "safe" speed.

   B. Use stab braking.

   C. Begin braking when you are 10 mph above your safe speed.

9. **The modulating control valve is?**

   A. A spring-loaded valve that will let you put the brakes on slowly if the service brakes fail.

   B. There is no such thing.

   C. It should not be used because it is very unsafe.

10. Which of the following will be true about your brake function if your anti lock braking system (ABS) fails?

    A. You will still have normal brake function and will just need to get the ABS repaired soon.

    B. It may cause problems with other mechanical systems and possibly pose a huge fire risk.

    C. It will slow your truck to a halt and force you to pull over.

    D. You will have no brake function, and your truck will be out of control.

11. Which of the following is not part of the braking process when you're driving a tractor-trailer combination vehicle with an antilock braking system (ABS)?

    A. Brake the same way no matter what you're driving: a vehicle with ABS, a vehicle with a trailer, or something else.

    B. You should monitor your tractor and trailer and ease off the brakes to keep control when you slow down.

    C. It would help if you used only the braking necessary to stay safely in control.

    D. It would help if you drove faster to be able to keep the trailer and tractor straight.

12. Which of the following are true about a dual air brake system?

    A. Usually, one system operates the front axle, and the other one operates the rear axle.

    B. It uses a single set of brake controls.

    C. One system is called the "primary" system, and the other is called the "secondary" system.

    D. All of the above is true.

13. How can you tell if your vehicle is equipped with an antilock braking system (ABS)?

    A. Check if the vehicle was manufactured after 2000.

    B. Check if the vehicle was manufactured after 2010.

    C. ABS is still optional.

    D. Check if the vehicle was manufactured after 1998.

14. Spring brakes are

    A. brakes that come on automatically on a truck or tractor when the psi drops too low.

    B. Made up of powerful springs that are held back by air pressure while you are driving.

    C. Not going to take full effect until your psi drops to a certain range, typically 20 to 30 psi.

    D. All of the above.

15. In the event of a brake system failure, the emergency brake system uses _____ to stop the vehicle.

    A. only the parking brakes

    B. parts of the service brakes and parking brakes

    C. only the service brakes

16. Repeatedly pressing and releasing (fanning) the brake pedal may result in

    A. a loss of brake air pressure.

    B. A buildup of brake air pressure.

    C. No change in brake air pressure.

17. **If the spring brakes are on, when should you push the brake pedal?**

    A. Only when driving downhill

    B. Never

    C. Only on a slippery road

18. **You'll know that your brakes are fading if**

    A. the brake feels spongy when you apply pressure.

    B. You release the brake pedal, and your speed increases.

    C. You have to press the brake pedal harder than usual to control your speed.

19. **A converter dolly with antilock brakes (ABS) is required to have**

    A. a yellow lamp on the left side.

    B. A white lamp on the left side.

    C. A white lamp on the right side.

20. **Which of the following is the most important thing about hard braking?**

    A. Disconnecting the steering axle brakes will help keep your vehicle in a straight line during emergency braking.

    B. Don't lock the wheels for longer than an instant.

    C. Never do it without downshifting first.

21. **In controlled braking, you**

    A. lock the wheels for short periods.

    B. Can turn sharply.

    C. Brake in a straight line.

22. **If oil and water collect in the air tanks, what could happen to the brakes?**

    A. The brakes could heat up.

    B. The brakes could lock up.

    C. The brakes could fail.

23. **S-cam drum brakes have an S-cam in each brake chamber. Why is it called an "S-cam?"**

    A. It is shaped like the letter "S."

    B. It makes the brake shoes move in an S-shaped path.

    C. It is constantly spinning whenever the wheel is spinning.

24. **To test the air service brakes,**

    A. stop the vehicle, put it in low gear, depress the brake pedal, and gently pull against the brakes.

    B. Brake firmly while slowly moving forward.

    C. Brake firmly while slowly moving backward.

25. **When can you leave your truck unattended without first applying the parking brakes or chocking the wheels?**

    A. Never

    B. If you will only be away from the truck for a few minutes

    C. If you will be conducting your pre-trip inspection

Air Brakes Practice Exam 3

1. **If your truck or bus has dual parking control valves, it means that you can use pressure from a separate tank to:**

   A. Release the spring brakes to move a short distance.

   B. Apply more brake pressure if the main tank is getting low.

   C. Stay parked without using up service air pressure.

2. **The brake pads should be _____ for the brakes to be on?**

   A. Worn 1/32 of an inch.

   B. Against the drum.

   C. Disconnected from the slack adjusters.

   D. Worn dangerously thin.

3. **You should know that your brakes are fading when:**

   A. You must push harder on the brake pedal to control your speed on a downgrade.

   B. The brake feels spongy when pressure is applied.

   C. Pressure on the brake pedal is released, and speed increases.

4. **The application pressure gauge shows the driver how much pressure:**

   A. Has been used on the trip.

   B. Is in the air tanks.

   C. Is being applied to the brakes.

5. **If the air compressor should develop a leak, what keeps the air in the tanks?**

   A. The tractor protection valve

   B. The emergency relay valve

   C. The one-way check valve

6. **Why drain water from the compressed air tanks?**

   A. The low boiling point of water reduces braking power.

   B. Water can freeze in cold weather and cause brake failure.

   C. Water over cools the compressor.

7. **During normal driving, spring brakes are usually held back by:**

   A. Air pressure

   B. Spring pressure

   C. Centrifugal force

8. **Brake drums must not have cracks longer than _____ the width of the friction area?**

   A. 1/8

   B. 1/4

   C. ½

9. **To test air leakage rate, the acceptable leakage rates per minute should be**

   A. 5 psi per minute for single vehicles and 6 psi per minute for combination vehicles.

   B. 5 psi per minute for single vehicles and 10 psi per minute for combination vehicles.

   C. 2 psi per minute for single vehicles and 3 psi per minute for combination vehicles.

   D. 1 psi per minute for single vehicles and 3 psi per minute for combination vehicles.

10. **How do brakes work on a long, steep downgrade?**

    A. They work as a supplement to the braking effect of your engine.

    B. Not applicable; no braking effect is involved in a downgrade.

    C. They work as the main braking mechanism.

    D. They work as the main braking mechanism with the engine braking effect as an emergency backup.

11. **How would you check your truck's slack adjusters?**

    A. Accelerate, then brake hard.

    B. Use gloves and pull hard on each slack adjuster you can reach.

    C. Press the brake pedal while listening for any strange noises.

    D. All of the above will work

12. **The parking brake control**

    A. applies the brakes during normal driving.

    B. Lets the air out of the brake chambers.

    C. Applies the brakes in the event of an emergency.

13. **If the low air pressure warning signal is not working,**

    A. it may lead to sudden emergency braking in a single-circuit air system.

    B. You may lose air pressure, but at least you'll know about it anyway.

    C. Neither of the above will happen.

14. **Your vehicle has a dual air brake system. One of the systems loses air pressure. What will happen?**

    A. The manual slack adjusters will not be set properly.

    B. The emergency brakes will come on immediately.

    C. Either the front or rear brakes will not be fully operational.

15. **Under ideal conditions, the average driver of a truck or bus equipped with air brakes and traveling at 55 mph would require what stopping distance?**

    A. 300 to 350 feet

    B. More than 400 feet

    C. 100 to 250 feet

16. **Modern air brake systems are three different systems combined: the service brakes, parking brakes, and _____ brakes.**

    A. S-cam

    B. emergency

    C. foot

17. **To check the free play of manual slack adjusters on S-cam brakes, you should:**

    A. Stop on level ground and apply the parking brakes.

    B. Park on level ground, chock the wheels and release the parking brakes.

    C. Park on level ground and drain off air pressure before adjusting.

18. **Your truck or bus has a dual air brake system. If a low air pressure warning comes on for only one system, what should you do?**

    A. Reduce your speed and drive to the nearest garage for repairs.

    B. Continue at normal speed and find a garage before the brakes lock.

    C. Stop. Safely park and continue only after the system is fixed.

19. **If your vehicle has an alcohol evaporator every day during cold weather, you should:**

    A. Check and fill in the alcohol level.

    B. Change the alcohol from a new bottle.

    C. Clean the air filter with alcohol

20. **With S-cam drum brakes, when the brake chamber fills with air, air pressure pushes the pushrod out, moving the _____ and thus rotating the _____.**

    A. slack adjuster; brake camshaft

    B. slack adjuster; tie rod

    C. brake camshaft; tie rod

21. **In which of the following situations should you NOT apply the parking brakes?**

    A. When you are testing whether they will hold the vehicle

    B. If the brakes are very hot

    C. If you're parking for less than one hour

22. **Which of the following can cause brakes to fail or fade?**

    A. Overheating, low air pressure, and not relying on the engine braking effect

    B. Not taking your foot off the accelerator

    C. Not pressing the brake pedal hard enough

23. **If you need to stop quickly and your vehicle lacks antilock brakes, you can use**

    A. the "controlled braking" method.

    B. The "stab braking" method.

    C. Either of the above.

24. **Tractor and straight truck spring brakes will come fully on when the air pressure drops to a range of**

    A. 60 to 80 psi.

    B. 20 to 45 psi.

    C. 10 to 15 psi.

25. **The modulating control valve allows you to control the**

    A. amount of pressure in the brake system.

    B. Front brakes.

    C. Spring brakes.

Air Brakes Practice Exam 4

1. **Air loss in a straight truck or bus should not be more than _____ with the engine off and the brakes applied.**

   A. 1 psi in 30 seconds

   B. 1 psi in one minute

   C. 3 psi in one minute

2. **What activates the stop switch?**

   A. Air pressure.

   B. Electrical.

   C. Mechanical force.

3. **A straight truck or bus air brake system should not leak at a rate of more than _____ psi per minute with the engine off and the brakes released.**

   A. 1

   B. 2

   C. 3

4. **Vehicles with air brakes must have:**

   A. At least two air tanks.

   B. An air pressure gauge to show the pressure available for braking.

   C. An air pressure gauge to show air used by the brake chambers for braking.

5. **Slack adjusters should not have any more than _____ of play?**

   A. 1/2 inch

   B. 1 inch

   C. 1-1/2 inches

6. **What is the best way to test your vehicle's low air pressure warning signal?**

   A. With the engine off, step on and off the brake pedal to lower the air pressure below 60 psi.

   B. Pump the brakes while your vehicle is fully on.

   C. Pump the brakes until the air pressure drops below 30 psi.

   D. Manually let the air out of your brakes and see if the signal comes on.

7. **Which vehicles must have low air pressure warning signals?**

   A. Vehicles built after 2005 must have low air pressure warning signals.

   B. All vehicles with air brakes currently in operation must have low air pressure warning signals.

   C. Vehicles built after 2010 must have low air pressure warning signals.

   D. None; low air pressure warning signals are optional.

8. **On a long or steep downgrade, once you have reached your "safe" speed, brake until you are traveling**

   A. 5 mph slower.

   B. 15 mph slower.

   C. 10 mph slower.

9. **To check the slack adjusters on S-cam drum brakes, you should first**

   A. stop on level ground and apply the parking brakes.

   B. Park on level ground and drain off the air pressure.

   C. Park on level ground, chock the wheels and release the parking brakes.

10. **Before starting down a hill, you should be in the proper gear**

    A. so you can coast downhill.

    B. So you only have to apply the brake just hard enough to feel a definite slowdown.

    C. So you can go through the gears on the way down.

11. **To apply the parking brakes under normal conditions,**

    A. be sure the air brake system is fully pressurized.

    B. Let the air out of the brake chambers.

    C. Turn off the engine.

12. **Slack adjusters are**

    A. between the power screw and pushrod on disc brakes.

    B. A part of the air brake system is used to adjust the brakes.

    C. Between the pushrod and S-cam on drum brakes.

    D. All of the above.

13. **Which of the following is NOT part of the air brake system?**

    A. Service brake system

    B. Parking brake system

    C. Emergency brake system

    D. Radio signal system

14. **Air braking takes more time than hydraulic braking because air brakes:**

    A. Use different brake drums.

    B. Need to have airflow through the lines to work.

    C. Require heavier return springs.

15. **In air brake vehicles, the parking brakes should be used:**

    A. Whenever the vehicle is parked.

    B. To hold your speed when going downhill.

    C. Only during pre and post-trip inspections.

16. **The brake pedal in an air brake system:**

    A. Controls the speed of the air compressor.

    B. Is to be used as a footrest during normal driving.

    C. Controls the air pressure applied to the brakes.

17. **Your vehicle has a dual air brake system; if a low air pressure warning comes on for the secondary system, you should?**

    A. Stop, safely park, and continue only when the system is fixed.

    B. Reduce your speed and test the remaining system while underway.

    C. Reduce your speed and drive to the nearest garage for repairs.

18. The tractor protection valve

    A. will close automatically if the air supply drops to a certain level.

    B. Will close if you apply the parking brakes.

    C. Provides the air supply for the brake system.

    D. Does all of the above.

19. What is the first thing you should do if the low air pressure warning comes on?

    A. Stop.

    B. Upshift.

    C. Downshift.

20. When should you use the parking brake?

    A. Only if you are away from your vehicle for an extended period of time

    B. Every time you leave your vehicle, with a few exceptions

    C. Only in urban areas where there are many other vehicles

    D. Every time you leave your vehicle for any length of time

21. The supply pressure gauge shows the driver how much pressure:

    A. Has been used in this trip.

    B. Is in the air tanks.

    C. Is being sent to the brake chambers.

22. Which of the following is NOT part of the drum brake?

    A. Slack adjuster

    B. Brake drum

    C. Return spring

    D. Safety valve

23. The safety release valve will blow at _____ psi?

    A. 120

    B. 150

    C. 160

24. In an emergency stop, you should?

    A. Use the hand valve and service brakes.

    B. Use the stab braking method

    C. Use the brakes hard without locking the wheels.

25. What are spring brakes?

    A. If the air brakes leak down, springs apply the brakes to stop the vehicle.

    B. They are the master brakes.

    C. They are the springs on the brake pedal.

Air Brakes Answers & Explained

Air Brakes Practice Exam 1
Answers & Explained

1. **Oil and water usually collect in compressed air tanks. If you do not have an automatic tank drain, when should you drain the air tanks?**

CORRECT ANSWER: After every working day.

EXPLANATION: If your vehicle does not have automatic air tank drains, drain your air tanks at the end of each working day to remove moisture and oil. Otherwise, the brakes could fail.

2. **What is the S-cam used for?**

CORRECT ANSWER: To apply the brakes.

EXPLANATION: When you push the brake pedal, air is let into each brake chamber. Air pressure pushes the rod out, moving the slack adjuster, thus twisting the brake camshaft. This turns the s-cam forcing the brake shoes away from one another and presses them against the inside of the brake drum.

3. **Which of the following makes the total stopping distance for air brakes longer than that for hydraulic brakes?**

CORRECT ANSWER: Brake lag distance.

EXPLANATION: With air brakes there is an added delay or Brake Lag. This is the time required for the brakes to work after the brake pedal is pushed. With hydraulic brakes, the brakes work instantly. With air brakes it takes a little time, one half second or more, for the air to flow through the lines to the brakes.

4. **The brake system that applies and releases the brakes when the driver uses the brake pedal is the:**

CORRECT ANSWER: Service brake system.

EXPLANATION: The service brake system applies and releases the brakes when you use the brake pedal during normal driving.

5. To make an emergency stop with air brakes, using the stab braking method, you should:

CORRECT ANSWER: Brake as hard as you can, get off the brakes when the wheels lock, get back on the brakes when the wheels start rolling again.

EXPLANATION: Stab braking means that you: apply your brakes all the way, and release brakes when wheels lock up. As soon as the wheels start rolling, apply the brakes fully again.

6. Brake lag distance at 55 mph is _____ feet?

CORRECT ANSWER: 32

EXPLANATION: The air brake lag distance at 55 mph on dry pavement adds about 32 feet.

7. If your vehicle has an alcohol evaporator, it is there to:

CORRECT ANSWER: Reduce the risk of ice in air brake valves in cold weather.

EXPLANATION: Some air brake systems have an alcohol evaporator to put alcohol into the air system. This helps to reduce the risk of ice in air brake valves and other parts during cold weather. Daily air tank drainage is still needed to get rid of water and oil.

8. What can legally hold a parking or emergency brake in position for a truck, truck tractor or bus?

CORRECT ANSWER: Spring pressure

EXPLANATION: All trucks, truck tractors, and buses must be equipped with emergency brakes and parking brakes. They must be held on by mechanical force because air pressure can eventually leak away. Spring brakes are usually used to meet these needs.

9. The braking power of the spring brakes:

CORRECT ANSWER: Depends on the adjustment of the service brakes.

EXPLANATION: The braking power of spring brakes depends on the brakes being in adjustment. If the brakes are not adjusted properly, neither the regular brakes nor the emergency/parking brakes will work right.

10. Which of the following should you do before leaving your vehicle unattended?

CORRECT ANSWER: Do all of the above.

EXPLANATION: Never leave your vehicle unattended without applying the parking brakes or chocking the wheels. Your vehicle might roll away and cause injury and damage.

11. Under which conditions are front wheel brakes good?

CORRECT ANSWER: All weather conditions

EXPLANATION: Front wheel brakes have been shown to be ideal under all weather and driving conditions. Front wheel braking is unlikely to cause a skid even on icy roads.

12. If the air tanks are not drained,

CORRECT ANSWER: your brakes may fail because of water freezing.

EXPLANATION: Compressed air usually has some water and some compressor oil in it, which is bad for the air brake system. For example, the water can freeze in cold weather and cause brake failure.

13. An antilock braking system (ABS)

CORRECT ANSWER: activates when your wheels are about to lock up.

EXPLANATION: ABS is a computerized system that keeps your wheels from locking up during hard brake applications.

14. Which of the following can cause brakes to fade or fail?

CORRECT ANSWER: All of the above

EXPLANATION: Brakes can fade or fail from excessive heat caused by using them too much and not relying on the engine braking effect.

15. What is the best way to test if your vehicle's spring brakes come on automatically?

CORRECT ANSWER: All of the above are correct.

EXPLANATION: On both tractor-trailers and single vehicles, to test whether the spring brakes will come on automatically, use the same method you use for testing the low air pressure warning signal: Step on and off the brake pedal, this time until you reach an even lower PSI reading and the parking brake valve closes or pops out.

16. If your vehicle has a properly functioning dual air brake system and minimum-sized air tanks, the air pressure should build from 85 to 100 psi within _____ seconds.

CORRECT ANSWER: 45

EXPLANATION: When the engine is at operating RPM's, the pressure should build from 85 to 100 psi within 45 seconds in dual air systems. If the vehicle has larger than minimum air tanks, the buildup time can be longer and still be safe.

17. The air compressor will stop pumping air into the air tanks at _____ psi.

CORRECT ANSWER: 125

EXPLANATION: The governor controls when the air compressor will pump air into the air storage tanks. When air tank pressure rises to the "cut-out" level around 125 psi, the governor stops the compressor from pumping air. When the tank pressure falls to the "cut-in" pressure around 100 psi, the governor allows the compressor to start pumping again.

18. Excessive heat caused by overuse of the service brakes can cause

CORRECT ANSWER: the brakes to fade.

EXPLANATION: Brakes can fade or fail from excessive heat caused by using them too much and not relying on the engine braking effect.

19. Excessive use of the service brakes may result in overheating, which can lead to

CORRECT ANSWER: expansion of the brake drums.

EXPLANATION: Brake fade results from excessive heat causing chemical changes in the brake lining, which reduce friction, and also causing expansion of the brake drums.

20. A typical air brake system is fully charged at

CORRECT ANSWER: 125 psi.

EXPLANATION: Pumping by the air compressor should start at about 100 psi and stop at about 125 psi.

21. During normal driving, spring brakes are usually held back by

CORRECT ANSWER: air pressure.

EXPLANATION: Parking or emergency brakes must be held on by mechanical force because air pressure can eventually leak away. Spring brakes are usually used to meet these needs. When driving, powerful springs are held back by air pressure.

22. During your final air brake check, if the air pressure does not build up fast enough,

CORRECT ANSWER: the air pressure may drop too low during driving.

EXPLANATION: If air pressure does not build up fast enough, your pressure may drop too low during driving, requiring an emergency stop. Don't drive until you get the problem fixed.

23. To test the static air leakage rate, you should

CORRECT ANSWER: turn off the engine, release the parking brake, and let the system settle.

EXPLANATION: With a fully-charged air system (typically 125 psi), turn off the engine, release the parking brake (push in); and time the air pressure drop.

24. Air brakes use _____ to make the brakes work.

CORRECT ANSWER: compressed air

EXPLANATION: Air brakes use compressed air to make the brakes work. Air brakes are a good and safe way of stopping large and heavy vehicles, but the brakes must be well maintained and used properly.

25. When you press the brake pedal,

CORRECT ANSWER: compressed air enters the brake chambers.

EXPLANATION: When you push the brake pedal, air is let into each brake chamber.

Air Brakes Practice Exam 2
Answers & Explained

1. The air compressor governor controls:

CORRECT ANSWER: When air is pumped into the air tanks.

EXPLANATION: The governor controls when the air compressor will pump air into the air storage tanks. When air tank pressure rises to the "cut-out" level around 125 psi, the governor stops the compressor from pumping air. When the tank pressure falls to the "cut-in" pressure around 100 psi, the governor allows the compressor to start pumping again.

2. Of the choices below, the first thing to do when a low air pressure warning comes on is:

CORRECT ANSWER: Stop and safely park as soon as possible.

EXPLANATION: When the low air pressure warning light and buzzer first come on, bring the vehicle to a safe stop right away, while you can still control the brakes.

3. Air brake equipped vehicles must have:

CORRECT ANSWER: A supply pressure gauge.

EXPLANATION: All vehicles with air brakes have a pressure gauge connected to the air tank. If the vehicle has a dual air brake system, there will be a gauge for each half of the system.

4. Modern air brake systems combine three different systems. They are the service brakes, the parking brakes, and the:

CORRECT ANSWER: Emergency brakes.

EXPLANATION: Air brakes are really three different braking systems: service brake, parking brake, and emergency brake.

5. If you must make an emergency stop, you should brake so that you:

CORRECT ANSWER: Stay in a straight line and can steer.

EXPLANATION: You should brake in a way that will keep your vehicle in a straight line and allow you to turn if it becomes necessary. You can use the "controlled braking" method or the "stab braking" method.

6. **The driver must be able to see a warning that is given before air pressure in the service air tanks falls below:**

CORRECT ANSWER: 60 psi

EXPLANATION: Low air warning devices (buzzer, light, flag) should activate before air pressure drops below 60 psi or the level specified by the manufacturer.

7. **The most common type of foundation brakes found on heavy vehicles is the:**

CORRECT ANSWER: S-cam brake

EXPLANATION: Wedge brakes and disc brakes are less common than s-cam brakes.

8. **When driving down a long steep hill you should:**

CORRECT ANSWER: Release the brake when you are 5 mph below your "safe" speed.

EXPLANATION: Snub braking method is used for steep downhill grades, in this method apply the brakes just hard enough to feel a definite slowdown. When your speed has been reduced to approximately 5 mph below your "safe" speed, release the brakes. When your speed has increased to your "safe" speed, repeat.

9. **The modulating control valve is?**

CORRECT ANSWER: A spring-loaded valve that will let you put on the brakes on slowly if the service brakes fail.

EXPLANATION: In some vehicles, a control handle on the dash board may be used to apply the spring brakes gradually. This is called a modulating valve. It is spring loaded, so you have a feel for the braking action. The more you move the control lever, the harder the spring brakes come on. They work this way, so you can control the spring brakes if the service brakes fail.

10. **Which of the following will be true about your brake function if your anti lock braking system (ABS) fails?**

CORRECT ANSWER: You will still have normal brake function and will just need to get the ABS repaired soon.

EXPLANATION: Without ABS you still have normal brake functions. Drive and brake as you always have.

11. Which of the following is not part of the braking process when you're driving a tractor-trailer combination vehicle with an antilock braking system (ABS)?

CORRECT ANSWER: You should drive faster so that you will be able to keep the trailer and tractor straight.

EXPLANATION: When you drive a vehicle with ABS, you should brake as you always have. In other words: use only the braking force necessary to stop safely and stay in control; brake the same way regardless of whether you have ABS on the bus, tractor, the trailer, or both; as you slow down monitor your tractor and trailer and back off the brakes if it is safe to do so to stay in control.

12. Which of the following are true about a dual air brake system?

CORRECT ANSWER: All of the above are true.

EXPLANATION: Most heavy-duty vehicles use dual air brake systems for safety. A dual air brake system has two separate air brake systems, which use a single set of brake controls. One system or primary system typically operates the regular brakes on the rear axle or axles. The other or secondary system operates the regular brakes on the front axle and possibly one rear axle.

13. How can you tell if your vehicle is equipped with an antilock braking system (ABS)?

CORRECT ANSWER: Check if the vehicle was manufactured after 1998.

EXPLANATION: The Department of Transportation requires that ABS be on air brake vehicles built on or after March 1, 1998.

14. Spring brakes are

CORRECT ANSWER: all of the above.

EXPLANATION: Spring brakes are an important backup system. Powerful springs that automatically apply the brakes if they sense that air pressure has been lost for some reason, such as a leak. They will also apply the brakes if the psi gets too low, although ideally, you should take control of your brakes before that happens.

15. In the event of a brake system failure, the emergency brake system uses _____ to stop the vehicle.

CORRECT ANSWER: parts of the service brakes and parking brakes

EXPLANATION: The emergency brake system uses parts of the service and parking brake systems to stop the vehicle in a brake system failure.

16. Repeatedly pressing and releasing (fanning) the brake pedal may result in

CORRECT ANSWER: a loss of brake air pressure.

EXPLANATION: Each time you release the brakes, some compressed air leaves the system and must be replenished by the air compressor. If you keep pressing and releasing the brake pedal, air may leave the system faster than the air compressor can replenish it, and the air pressure may drop to the point that the brakes won't work.

17. If the spring brakes are on, when should you push the brake pedal?

CORRECT ANSWER: Never

EXPLANATION: Never push the brake pedal down when the spring brakes are on. If you do, the brakes could be damaged by the combined forces of the springs and the air pressure.

18. You'll know that your brakes are fading if

CORRECT ANSWER: you have to press the brake pedal harder than usual to control your speed.

EXPLANATION: As the overheated drums expand, the brake shoes and linings have to move farther to contact the drums, and the force of this contact is reduced. So, you will be pressing harder on the pedal.

19. A converter dolly with antilock brakes (ABS) is required to have

CORRECT ANSWER: a yellow lamp on the left side.

EXPLANATION: Converter dollies built on or after March 1, 1998, are required to have antilock brakes. These dollies will have a yellow lamp on the left side of the dolly.

20. Which of the following is the most important thing about hard braking?

CORRECT ANSWER: Don't lock the wheels for longer than an instant.

EXPLANATION: Emergency braking does not mean pushing down on the brake pedal as hard as you can. That will only keep the wheels locked up and cause a skid. If the wheels are skidding, you cannot control the vehicle.

21. In controlled braking, you

CORRECT ANSWER: brake in a straight line.

EXPLANATION: You apply the brakes as hard as you can without locking the wheels. Keep steering wheel movements very small while doing this. If you need to make a larger steering adjustment or if the wheels lock, release the brakes. Re-apply the brakes as soon as you can.

22. If oil and water collects in the air tanks, what could happen to the brakes?

CORRECT ANSWER: The brakes could fail.

EXPLANATION: Compressed air usually has some water and some compressor oil in it, which is bad for the air brake system. For example, the water can freeze in cold weather and cause brake failure.

23. S-cam drum brakes have an S-cam in each brake chamber. Why is it called an "S-cam?"

CORRECT ANSWER: It is shaped like the letter "S."

EXPLANATION: The S-cam is S-shaped. The s-cam forces the brake shoes away from one another and presses them against the inside of the brake drum.

24. To test the air service brakes,

CORRECT ANSWER: brake firmly while slowly moving forward.

EXPLANATION: Pull forward at 5 mph, apply the service brake and stop. Check to see that the vehicle does not pull to either side and that it stops when the brake is applied.

25. When can you leave your truck unattended without first applying the parking brakes or chocking the wheels?

CORRECT ANSWER: Never

EXPLANATION: Never leave your vehicle unattended without applying the parking brakes or chocking the wheels. Your vehicle might roll away and cause injury and damage.

Air Brakes Practice Exam 3

Answers & Explained

1. **If your truck or bus has dual parking control valves it means that you can use pressure from a separate tank to:**

CORRECT ANSWER: Release the spring brakes to move a short distance.

EXPLANATION: When main air pressure is lost, the spring brakes come on. Some vehicles have a separate air tank which can be used to release the spring brakes. This is so you can move the vehicle in an emergency.

2. **The brake pads should be _____ for the brakes to be on?**

CORRECT ANSWER: Against the drum.

EXPLANATION: To stop, the brake shoes and linings are pushed against the inside of the drum. This causes friction, which slows the vehicle.

3. **You should know that your brakes are fading when:**

CORRECT ANSWER: You must push harder on the brake pedal to control your speed on a downgrade.

EXPLANATION: Increasing application pressure to hold the same speed means the brakes are fading.

4. **The application pressure gauge shows the driver how much pressure:**

CORRECT ANSWER: Is being applied to the brakes.

EXPLANATION: Application Pressure Gauge shows how much air pressure you are applying to the brakes.

5. **If the air compressor should develop a leak, what keeps the air in the tanks?**

CORRECT ANSWER: The one-way check valve

EXPLANATION: Installed on the compressor side of the air tank is a one-way check valve; it allows air into the tanks, but does not allow it to flow back to the compressor.

6. **Why drain water from the compressed air tanks?**

CORRECT ANSWER: Water can freeze in cold weather and cause brake failure.

EXPLANATION: Compressed air usually has some water and some compressor oil in it, which is bad for the air brake system, the water can freeze in cold weather and cause brake failure. The water and oil tend to collect in the bottom of the air tank. Be sure that you drain the air tanks completely.

7. During normal driving, spring brakes are usually held back by:

CORRECT ANSWER: Air pressure

EXPLANATION: When driving, powerful springs are held back by air pressure. If the air pressure is removed, the springs put on the brakes.

8. Brake drums must not have cracks longer than _____ the width of the friction area?

CORRECT ANSWER: 1/2

EXPLANATION: Brake drums or discs must not have cracks longer than 1/2 the width of the friction area.

9. To test air leakage rate, the acceptable leakage rates per minute should be

CORRECT ANSWER: 2 psi per minute for single vehicles and 3 psi per minute for combination vehicles.

EXPLANATION: The loss rate should be less than two psi in one minute for single vehicles and less than three psi in one minute for combination vehicles.

10. How do brakes work on a long, steep downgrade?

CORRECT ANSWER: They work as a supplement to the braking effect of your engine.

EXPLANATION: The use of brakes on a long and/or steep downgrade is only a supplement to the braking effect of the engine.

11. How would you check your truck's slack adjusters?

CORRECT ANSWER: Use gloves and pull hard on each slack adjuster you can reach.

EXPLANATION: Use gloves and pull hard on each slack adjuster that you can reach. If a slack adjuster moves more than about one inch where the push rod attaches to it, it probably needs adjustment.

12. The parking brake control

CORRECT ANSWER: lets the air out of the brake chambers.

EXPLANATION: A parking brake control in the cab allows the driver to let the air out of the spring brakes. This lets the springs put the brakes on.

13. If the low air pressure warning signal is not working,

CORRECT ANSWER: it may lead to sudden emergency braking in a single-circuit air system.

EXPLANATION: If the warning signal doesn't work, you could lose air pressure and you would not know it. This could cause sudden emergency braking in a single-circuit air system. In dual systems the stopping distance will be increased. Only limited braking can be done before the spring brakes come on.

14. Your vehicle has a dual air brake system. One of the systems loses air pressure. What will happen?

CORRECT ANSWER: Either the front or rear brakes will not be fully operational.

EXPLANATION: A dual air brake system has two separate air brake systems, which use a single set of brake controls. Each system has its own air tanks, hoses, lines, etc. One system typically operates the regular brakes on the rear axle or axles. The other system operates the regular brakes on the front axle and possibly one rear axle.

15. Under ideal conditions, the average driver of a truck or bus equipped with air brakes and traveling at 55 mph would require what stopping distance?

CORRECT ANSWER: More than 400 feet

EXPLANATION: The total minimum distance your vehicle has traveled, in ideal conditions; with everything considered, including perception distance, reaction distance and braking distance, until you can bring your vehicle to a complete stop. At 55 mph, your vehicle will travel about 450 feet.

16. Modern air brake systems are three different systems combined: the service brakes, parking brakes, and _____ brakes.

CORRECT ANSWER: emergency

EXPLANATION: Air brakes are really three different braking systems: service brake, parking brake, and emergency brake.

17. To check the free play of manual slack adjusters on S-cam brakes you should:

CORRECT ANSWER: Park on level ground, chock the wheels, and release the parking brakes.

EXPLANATION: If a slack adjuster moves more than about one inch where the push rod attaches to it, it probably needs adjustment.

18. Your truck or bus has a dual air brake system. If a low air pressure warning comes on for only one system, what should you do?

CORRECT ANSWER: Stop. Safely park and continue only after the system is fixed.

EXPLANATION: The warning light and buzzer should come on before the air pressure drops below 60 psi in either system. If this happens while driving, you should stop right away and safely park the vehicle. If one air system is very low on pressure, either the front or the rear brakes will not be operating fully. This means it will take you longer to stop. Bring the vehicle to a safe stop and have the air brakes system fixed.

19. If your vehicle has an alcohol evaporator, every day during cold weather you should:

CORRECT ANSWER: Check and fill the alcohol level.

EXPLANATION: Check the alcohol container and fill up as necessary, every day during cold weather.

20. With S-cam drum brakes, when the brake chamber fills with air, air pressure pushes the push rod out, moving the _____ and thus rotating the _____.

CORRECT ANSWER: slack adjuster; brake camshaft

EXPLANATION: In S-cam brakes when you push the brake pedal, air is let into each brake chamber. Air pressure pushes the rod out, moving the slack adjuster, thus twisting the brake camshaft. This turns the s-cam. The s-cam forces the brake shoes away from one another and presses them against the inside of the brake drum.

21. In which of the following situations should you NOT apply the parking brakes?

CORRECT ANSWER: If the brakes are very hot

EXPLANATION: Don't use the parking brakes if the brakes are very hot (from just having come down a steep grade), or if the brakes are very wet in freezing temperatures. If they are used while they are very hot, they can be damaged by the heat. If they are used in freezing temperatures when the brakes are very wet, they can freeze so the vehicle cannot move. Use wheel chocks instead.

22. Which of the following can cause brakes to fail or fade?

CORRECT ANSWER: Overheating, low air pressure, and not relying on the engine braking effect

EXPLANATION: Brakes can fade or fail from excessive heat caused by using them too much and not relying on the engine braking effect, they are also affected by adjustment, and low air pressure.

23. If you need to stop quickly and your vehicle lacks anti lock brakes, you can use

CORRECT ANSWER: either of the above.

EXPLANATION: You should brake in a way that will keep your vehicle in a straight line and allow you to turn if it becomes necessary. You can use the "controlled braking" method or the "stab braking" method.

24. Tractor and straight truck spring brakes will come fully on when the air pressure drops to a range of

CORRECT ANSWER: 20 to 45 psi.

EXPLANATION: Tractor and straight truck spring brakes will come fully on when air pressure drops to a range of 20 to 45 psi (typically 20 to 30 psi).

25. The modulating control valve allows you to control the

CORRECT ANSWER: spring brakes.

EXPLANATION: In some vehicles a control handle on the dash board may be used to apply the spring brakes gradually. This is called a modulating valve. It is spring-loaded, so you have a feel for the braking action. The more you move the control lever, the harder the spring brakes come on.

Air Brakes Practice Exam 4

Answers & Explained

1. **Air loss in a straight truck or bus should not be more than _____ with the engine off and the brakes applied.**

CORRECT ANSWER: 3 psi in one minute

EXPLANATION: With a fully-charged air system, turn off the engine, release the parking brake, and time the air pressure drop. The loss rate should be less than two psi in one minute for a single vehicle, brakes released, and three psi in one minute with the brakes applied.

2. **What activates the stop switch?**

CORRECT ANSWER: Air pressure.

EXPLANATION: Drivers behind you must be warned when you put your brakes on. The air brake system does this with an electric switch that works by air pressure. The switch turns on the brake lights when you put on the air brakes.

3. **A straight truck or bus air brake system should not leak at a rate of more than ____ psi per minute with the engine off and the brakes released.**

CORRECT ANSWER: 2

EXPLANATION: With a fully-charged air system, turn off the engine, release the parking brake, and time the air pressure drop. The loss rate should be less than two psi in one minute for a single vehicle, brakes released, and three psi in one minute with the brakes applied.

4. **Vehicles with air brakes must have:**

CORRECT ANSWER: An air pressure gauge to show the pressure available for braking.

EXPLANATION: All vehicles with air brakes have a pressure gauge connected to the air tank. If the vehicle has a dual air brake system, there will be a gauge for each half of the system.

5. **Slack adjusters should not have any more than _____ of play.**

CORRECT ANSWER: 1 inch

EXPLANATION: Park on level ground and chock the wheels to prevent the vehicle from moving, release the parking brakes so you can move the slack adjusters, using gloves and pull hard on each slack adjuster that you can reach, and if a slack adjuster moves more than about one inch where the push rod attaches to it then adjustments are needed.

6. What is the best way to test your vehicle's low air pressure warning signal?

CORRECT ANSWER: With the engine off, step on and off the brake pedal to lower the air pressure below 60 psi.

EXPLANATION: Shut the engine off when you have enough air pressure so that the low-pressure warning signal is not on. Turn the electrical power on and step on and off the brake pedal to reduce air tank pressure. The low air pressure warning signal must come on before the pressure drops to less than 60 psi in the air tank.

7. Which vehicles must have low air pressure warning signals?

CORRECT ANSWER: All vehicles with air brakes currently in operation must have low air pressure warning signals.

EXPLANATION: A low air pressure warning signal is required on vehicles with air brakes.

8. On a long or steep downgrade, once you have reached your "safe" speed, brake until you are traveling

CORRECT ANSWER: 5 mph slower.

EXPLANATION: Snub braking method is used for steep downhill grades, in this method apply the brakes just hard enough to feel a definite slowdown. When your speed has been reduced to approximately five mph below your "safe" speed, release the brakes. When your speed has increased to your "safe" speed, repeat.

9. To check the slack adjusters on S-cam drum brakes, you should first

CORRECT ANSWER: park on level ground, chock the wheels, and release the parking brakes.

EXPLANATION: To check slack adjusters on S-cam Brakes, park on level ground and chock the wheels to prevent the vehicle from moving and apply the parking brake.

10. Before starting down a hill, you should be in the proper gear

CORRECT ANSWER: so you only have to apply the brake just hard enough to feel a definite slowdown.

EXPLANATION: The use of brakes on a long and/or steep downgrade is only a supplement to the braking effect of the engine. Once the vehicle is in the proper low gear you should only have to apply the brakes just hard enough to feel a definite slowdown.

11. To apply the parking brakes under normal conditions,

CORRECT ANSWER: let the air out of the brake chambers.

EXPLANATION: A parking brake control in the cab allows the driver to let the air out of the spring brakes. This lets the springs put the brakes on.

12. Slack adjusters are

CORRECT ANSWER: all of the above.

EXPLANATION: Slack adjusters are an important part of your air brake system that allows you to adjust the brakes to ensure that they are safe. They are located in different places, depending on the type of brakes that you have.

13. Which of the following is NOT part of the air brake system?

CORRECT ANSWER: Radio signal system

EXPLANATION: Air brakes are really three different braking systems: service brake, parking brake, and emergency brake.

14. Air braking takes more time than hydraulic braking because air brakes:

CORRECT ANSWER: Need to have airflow through the lines to work.

EXPLANATION: With air brakes there is an added delay called Brake Lag. This is the time required for the brakes to work after the brake pedal is pushed.

15. In air brake vehicles, the parking brakes should be used:

CORRECT ANSWER: Whenever the vehicle is parked.

EXPLANATION: Any time you park use the parking brakes. Pull the parking brake control knob out to apply the parking brakes, push it in to release.

16. The brake pedal in an air brake system:

CORRECT ANSWER: Controls the air pressure applied to the brakes.

EXPLANATION: You put on the brakes by pushing down the brake pedal. Pushing the pedal down harder applies more air pressure. Letting up on the brake pedal reduces the air pressure and releases the brakes.

17. Your vehicle has a dual air brake system; if a low air pressure warning comes on for the secondary system, you should?

CORRECT ANSWER: Stop, safely park, and continue only when the system is fixed.

EXPLANATION: Even if the low-pressure alarm is for the secondary system you need to stop at a safe location, park, and get the issue fixed. It is unsafe for the vehicle to remain in motion with a low air alarm.

18. The tractor protection valve

CORRECT ANSWER: does all of the above.

EXPLANATION: The tractor protection valve keeps air in the tractor or truck brake system should the trailer break away or develop a bad leak, and it will close automatically if air pressure is low (typically 20-45 psi).

19. What is the first thing you should do if the low air pressure warning comes on?

CORRECT ANSWER: Stop.

EXPLANATION: If the low air pressure warning comes on, stop and safely park your vehicle as soon as possible.

20. When should you use the parking brake?

CORRECT ANSWER: Every time you leave your vehicle, with a few exceptions

EXPLANATION: Never leave your vehicle unattended without applying the parking brakes or chocking the wheels. Your vehicle might roll away and cause injury and damage. Exceptions are when the brakes are very hot, or wet and it is very cold outside. In this case use wheel chocks.

21. The supply pressure gauge shows the driver how much pressure:

CORRECT ANSWER: Is in the air tanks.

EXPLANATION: All vehicles with air brakes have a pressure gauge connected to the air tank, and it tells you how much pressure is in the air tanks.

22. Which of the following is NOT part of the drum brake?

CORRECT ANSWER: Safety valve

EXPLANATION: Drum brakes are on each of your vehicle's axles and contain about 10 different parts, including the axle, slack adjuster, and brake drum itself. While a safety valve is part of the air brake system, it is not part of the drum brake.

23. The safety release valve will blow at _____ psi?

CORRECT ANSWER: 150

EXPLANATION: A safety relief valve is installed in the first tank the air compressor pumps air to. The safety valve protects the tank and the rest of the system from too much pressure. The valve is usually set to open at 150 psi. If the safety valve releases air, something is wrong. Have the fault fixed by a mechanic.

24. In an emergency stop, you should?

CORRECT ANSWER: Use the stab braking method

EXPLANATION: Stab braking means that you: apply your brakes all the way, and release brakes when wheels lock up. As soon as the wheels start rolling, apply the brakes fully again.

25. What are spring brakes?

CORRECT ANSWER: If the air brakes leak down, springs apply the brakes to stop the vehicle.

EXPLANATION: When driving, powerful springs are held back by air pressure. If the air pressure is removed, the springs put on the brakes. A leak in the air brake system, which causes all the air to be lost, will also cause the springs to put on the brakes.

Notes

www.ingramcontent.com/pod-product-compliance
Lightning Source LLC
Chambersburg PA
CBHW081012120626
46546CB00010B/3119